ADULT COLORING BOOK

Stress Relieving Animal Designs

This Coloring Book Belongs To :

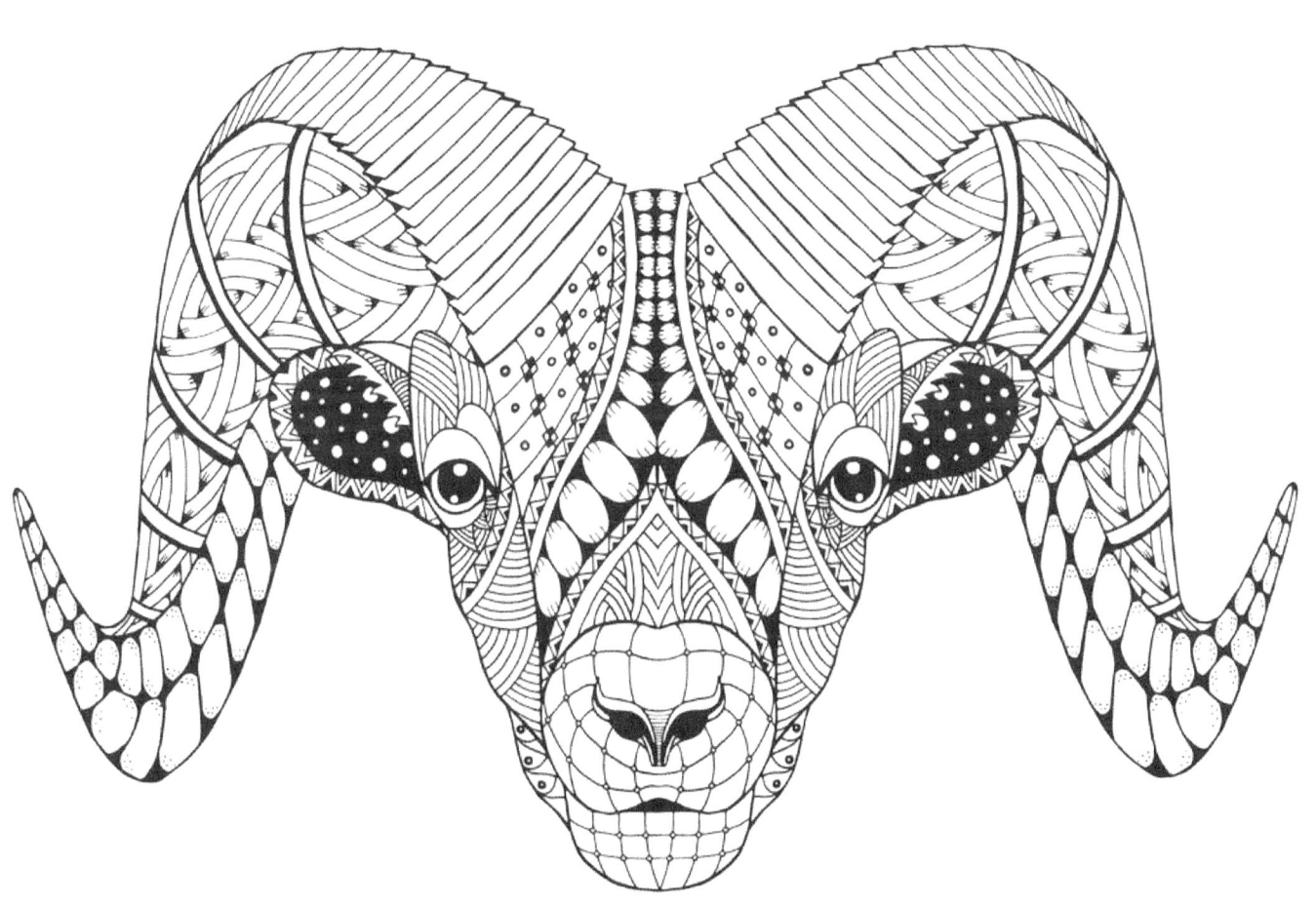

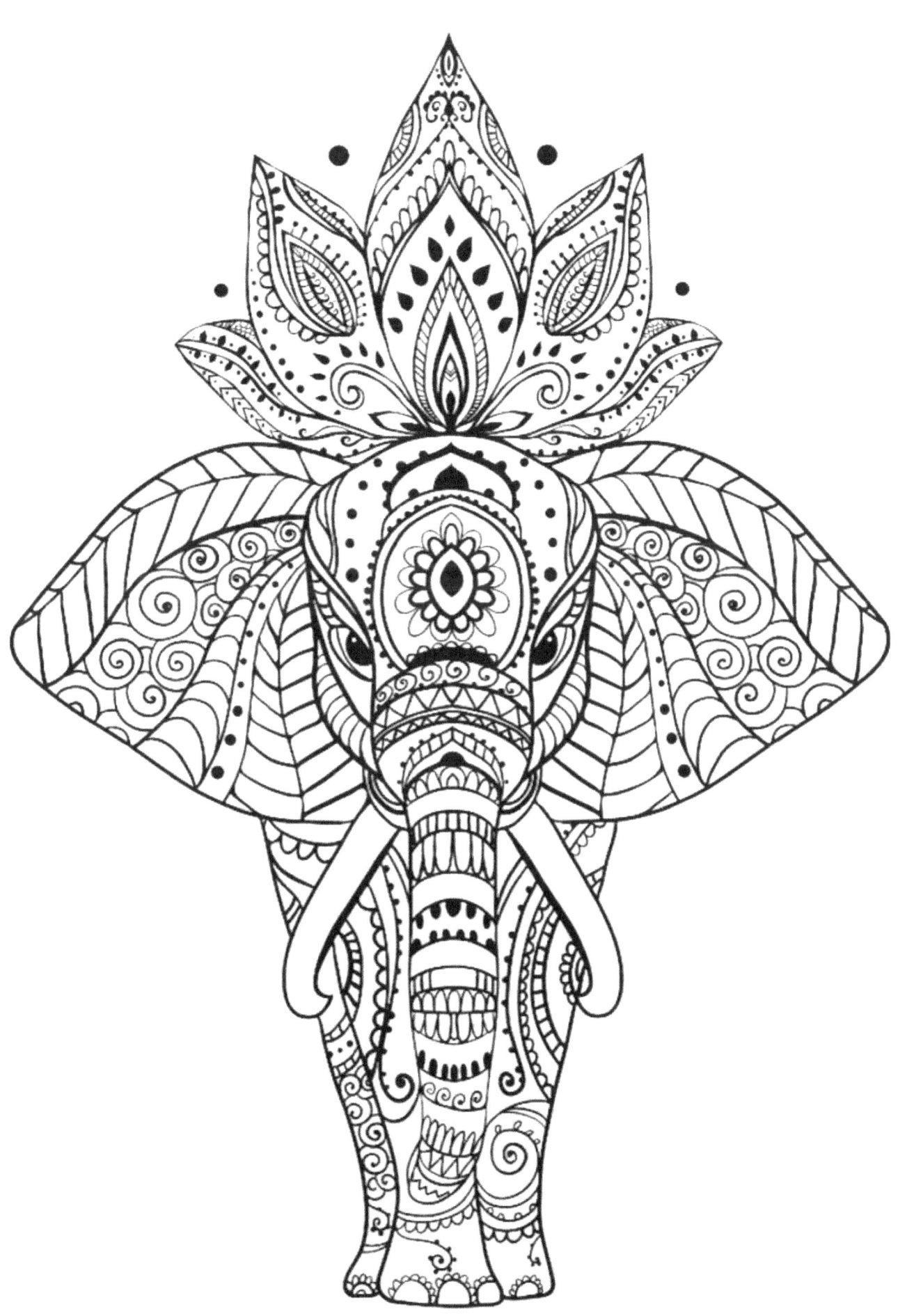

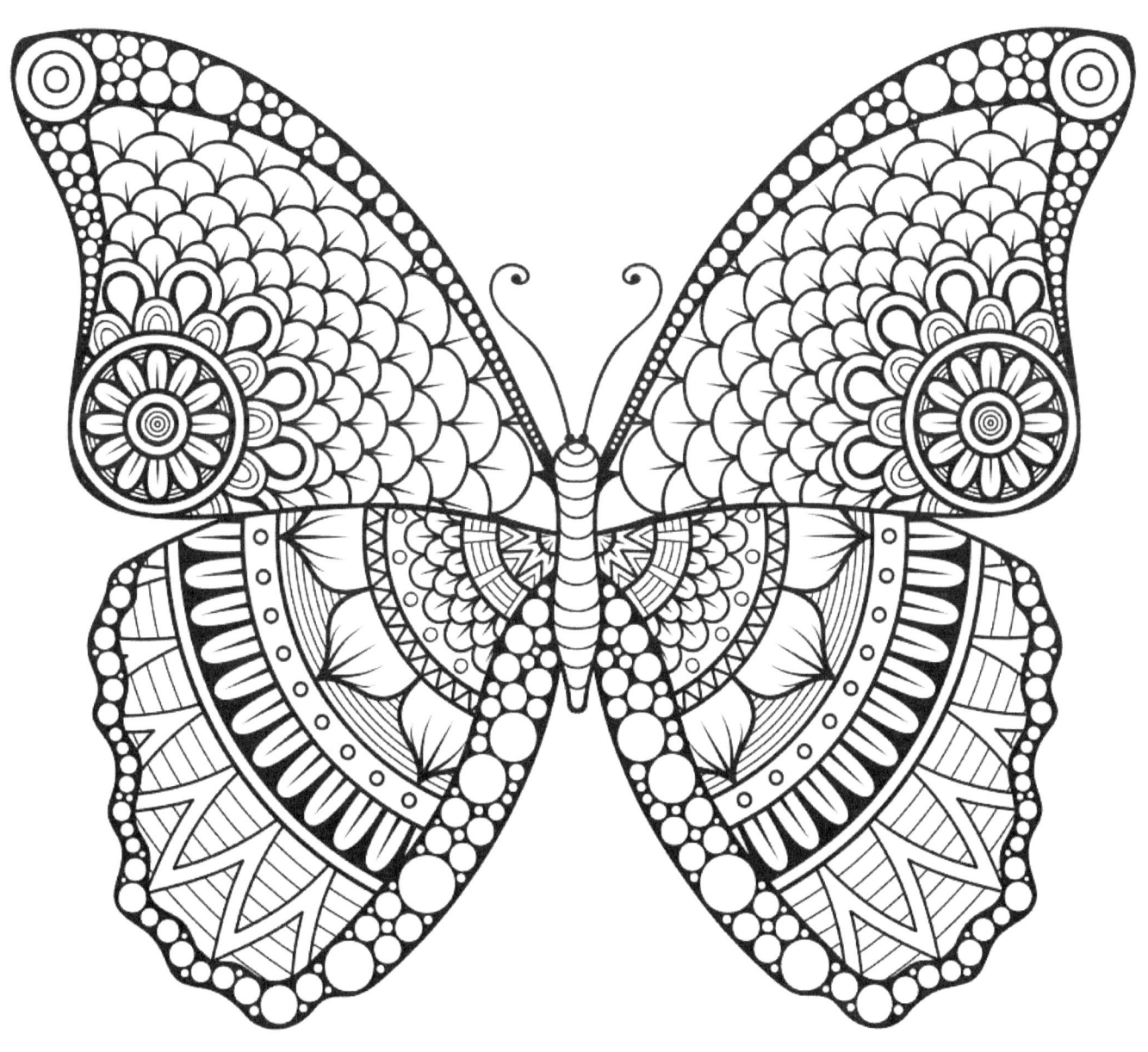

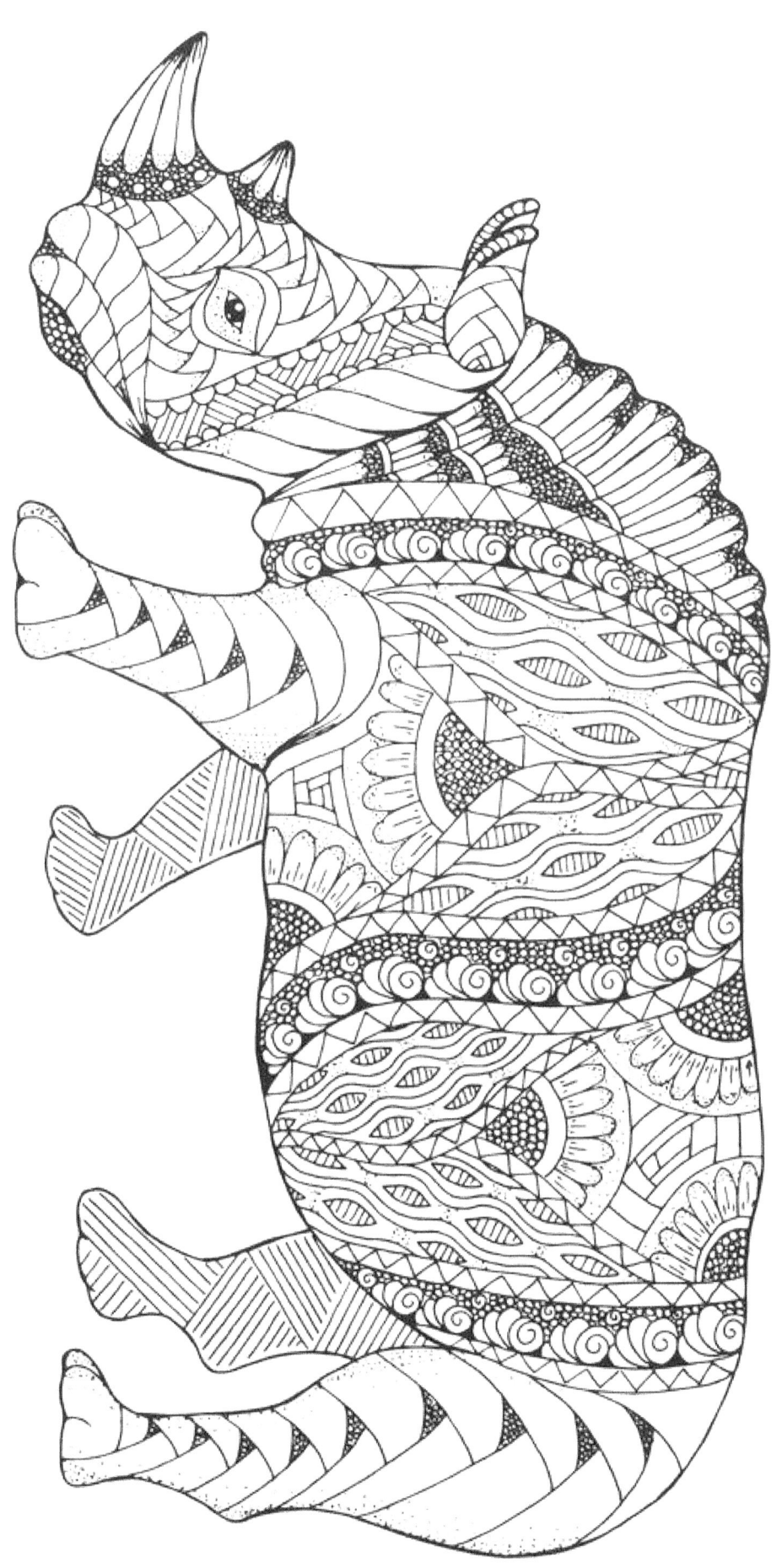

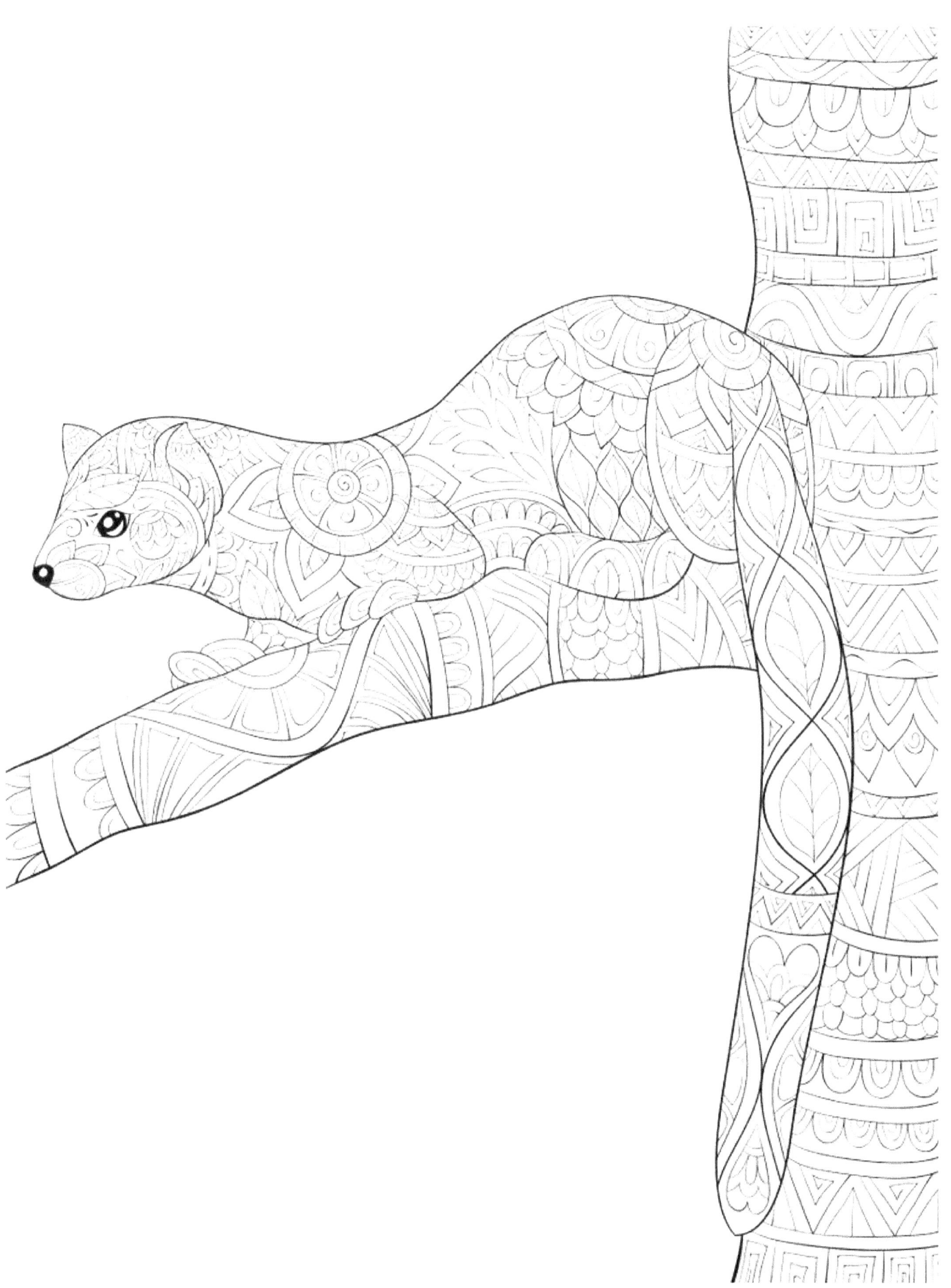

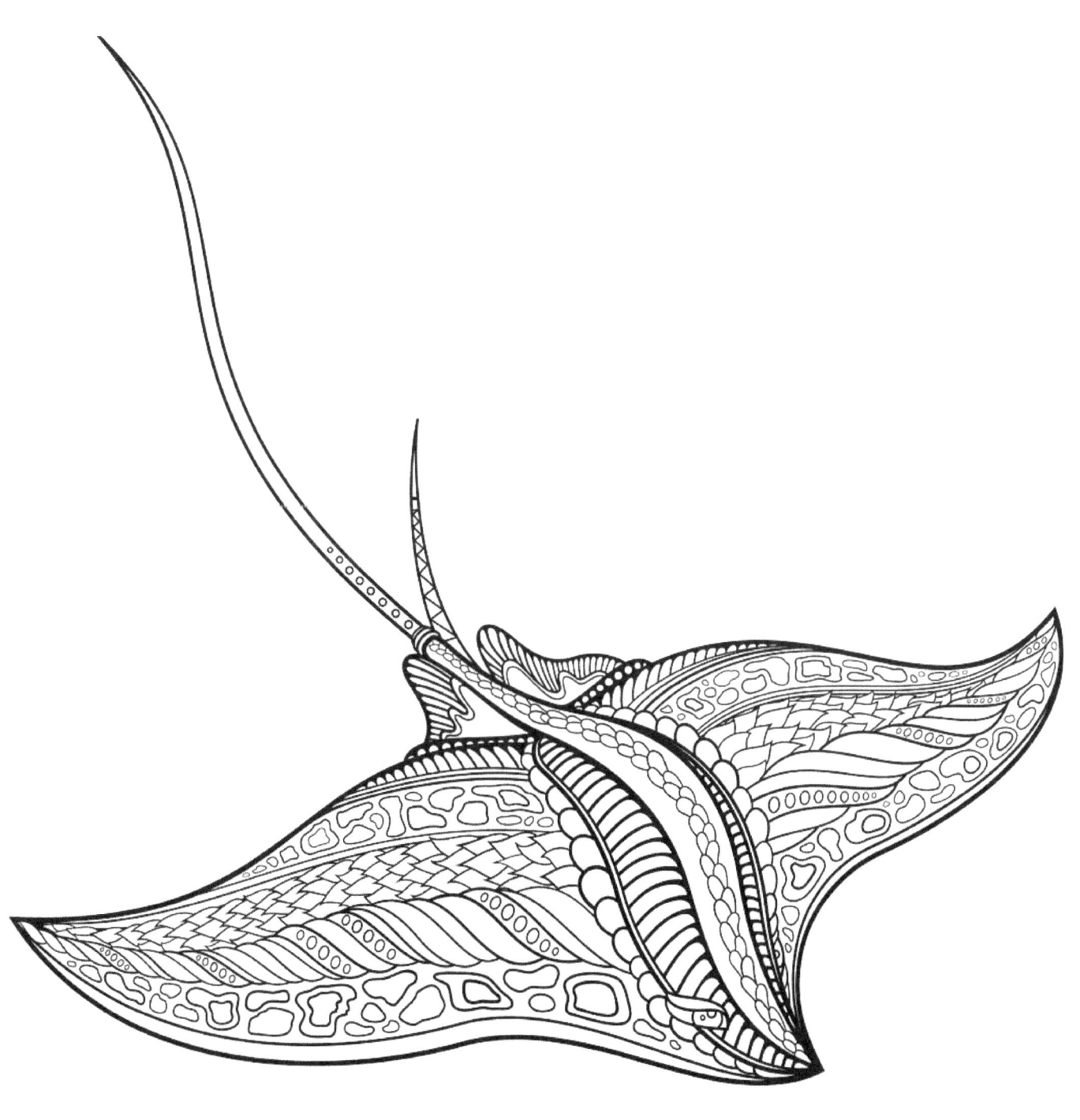

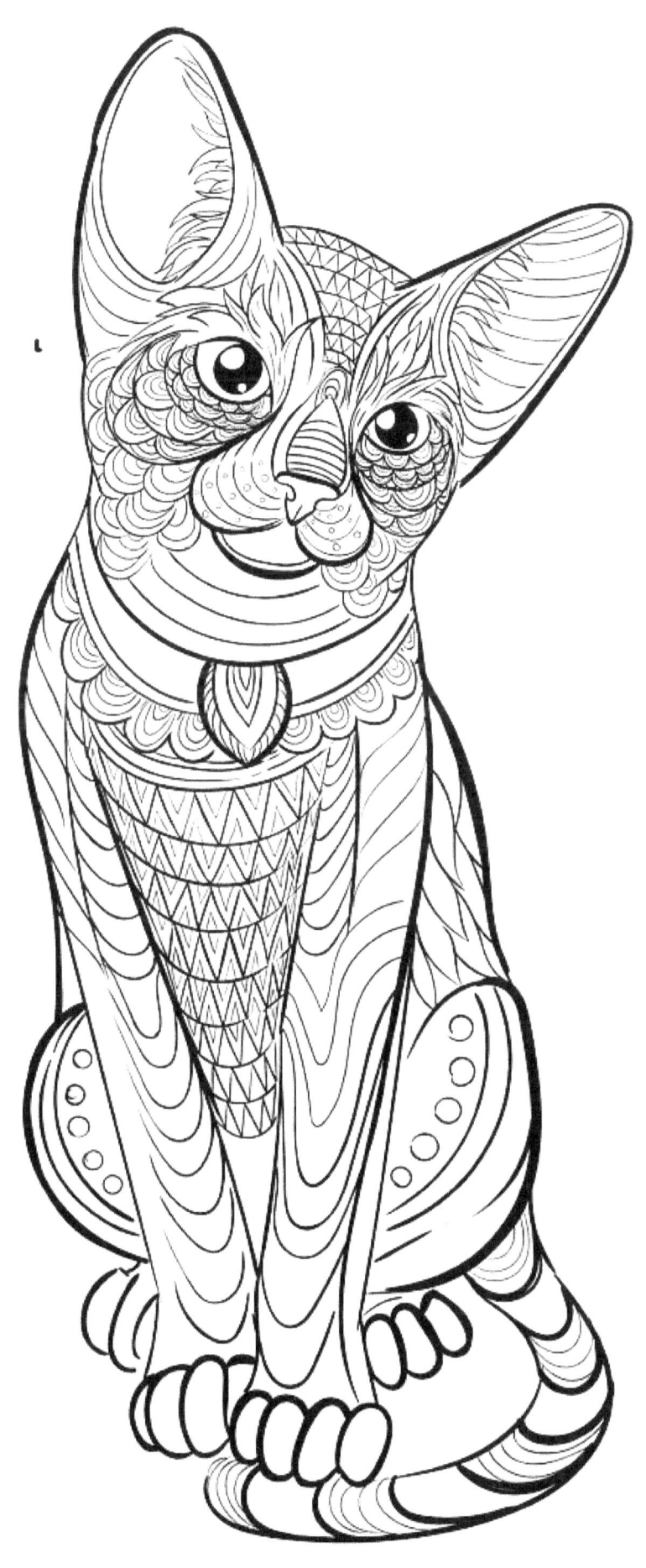

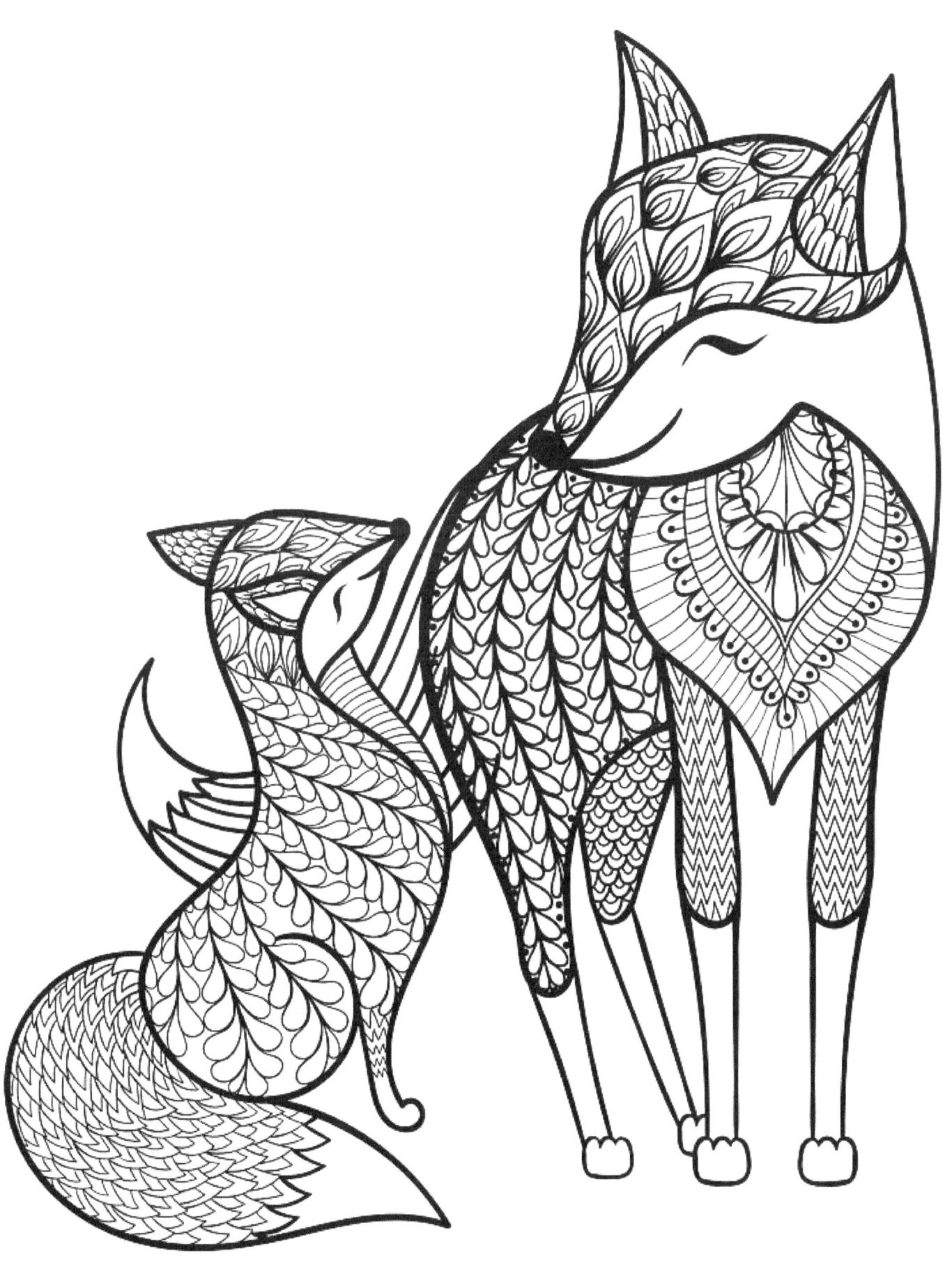

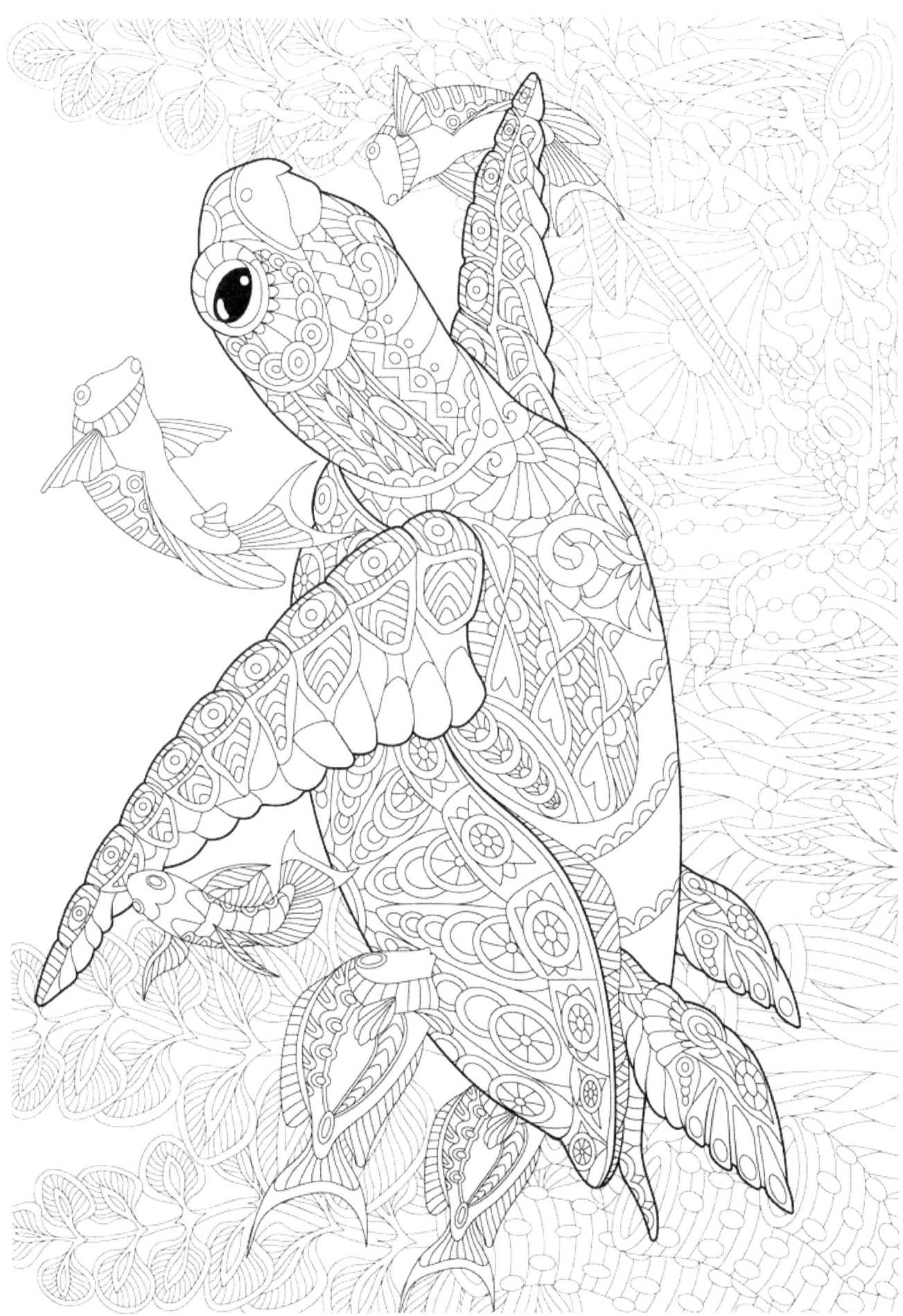

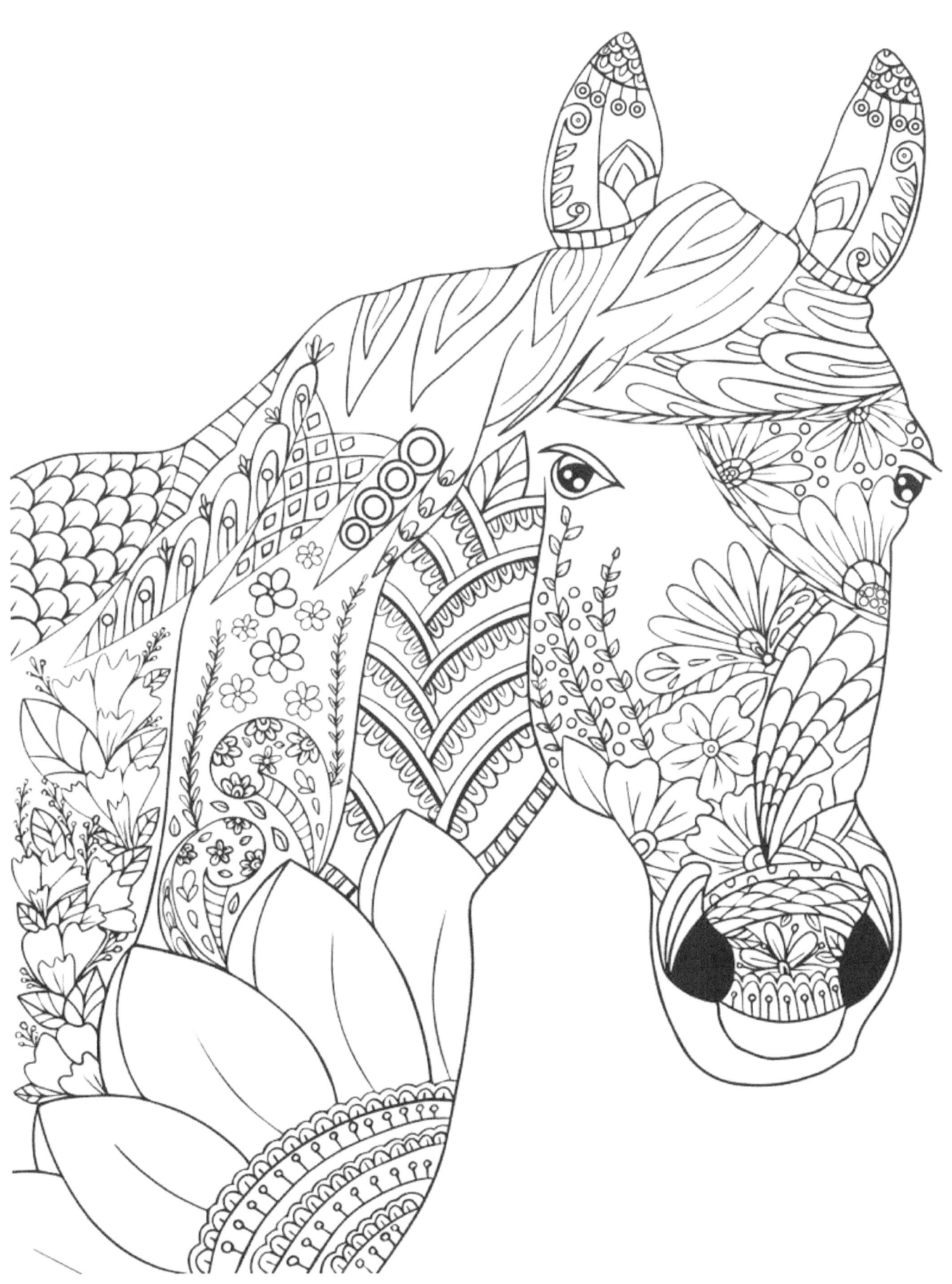

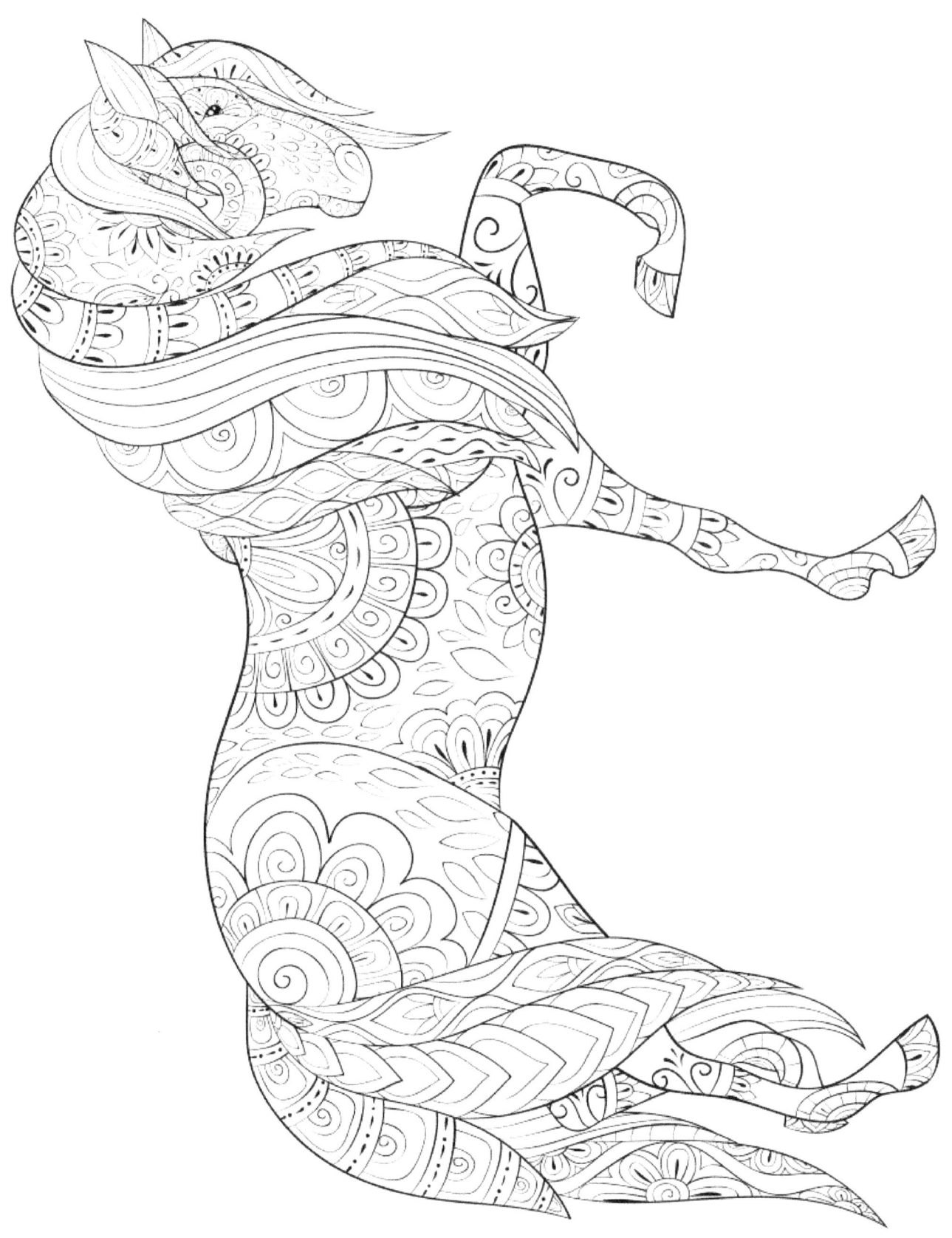

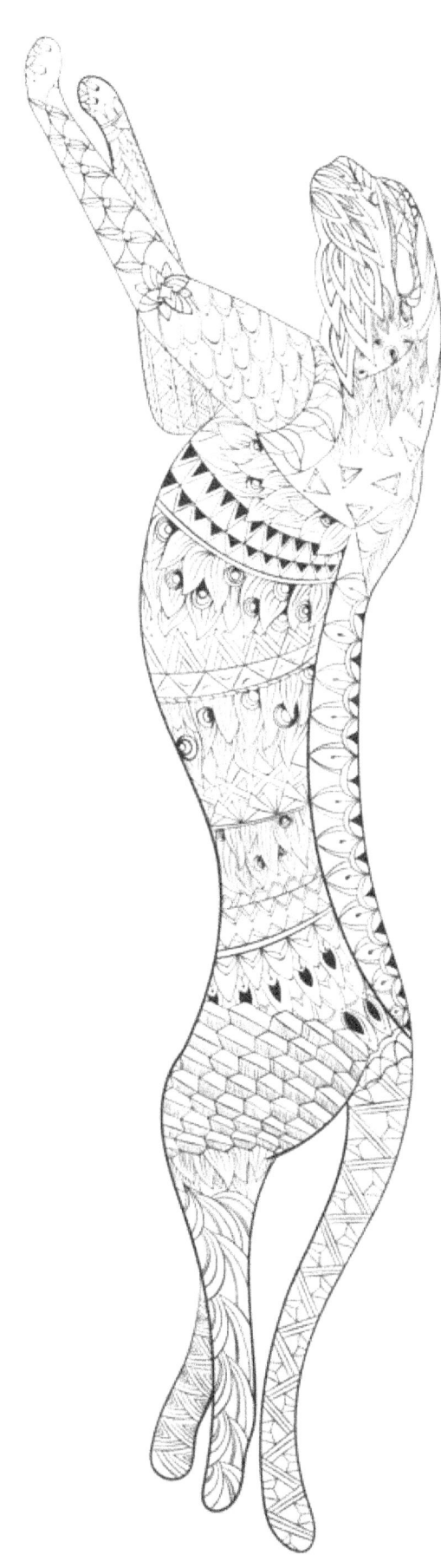

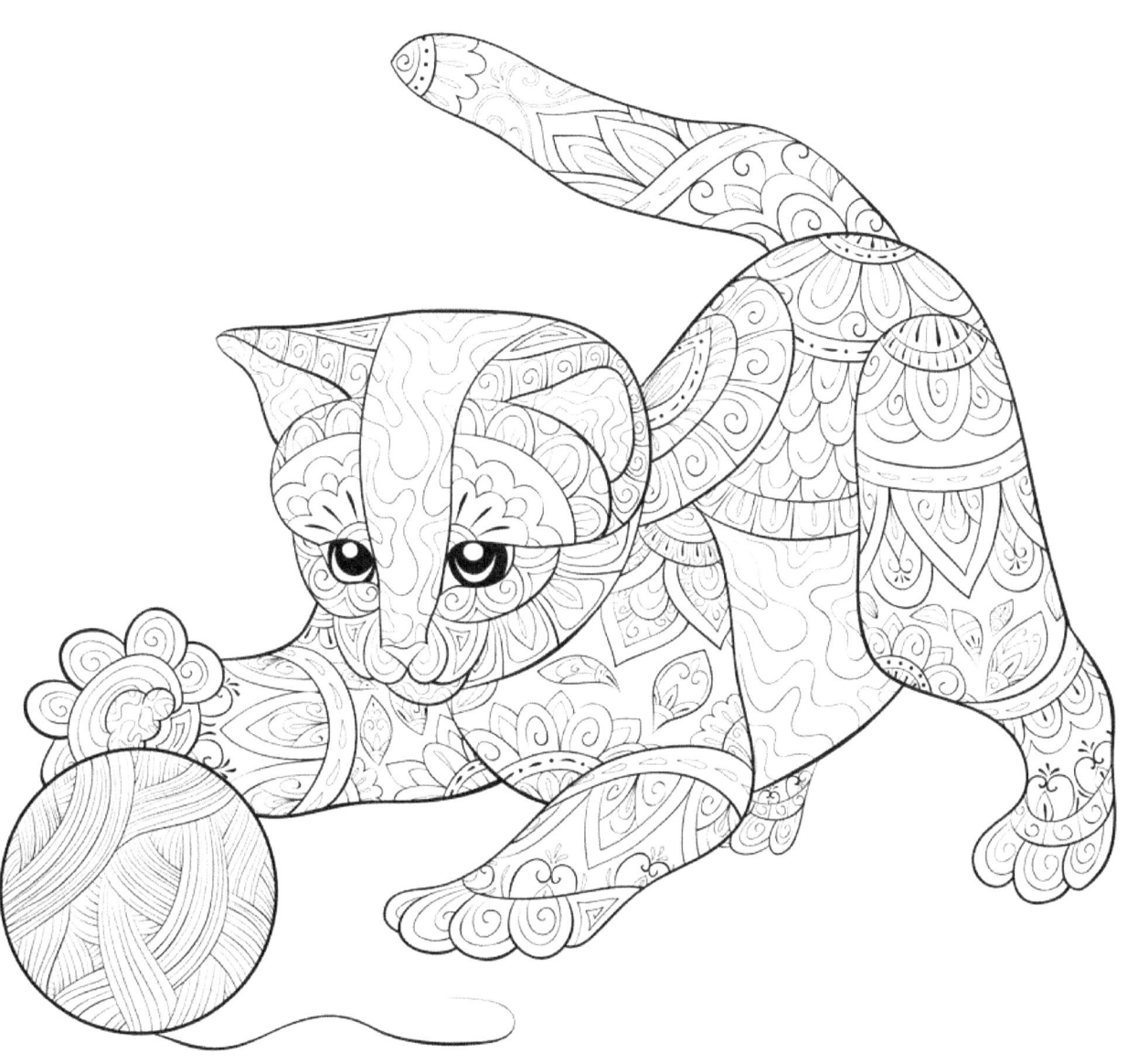

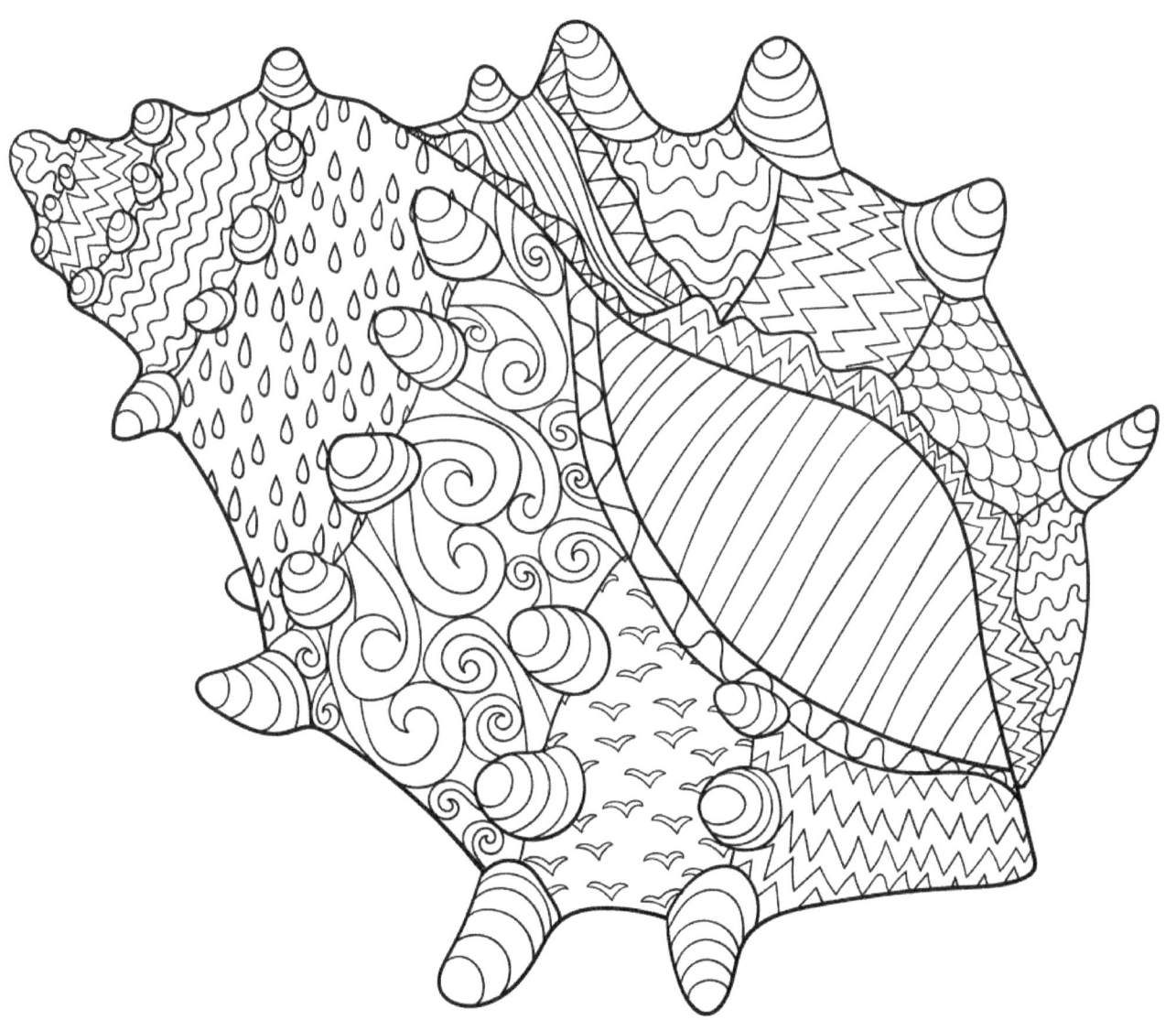

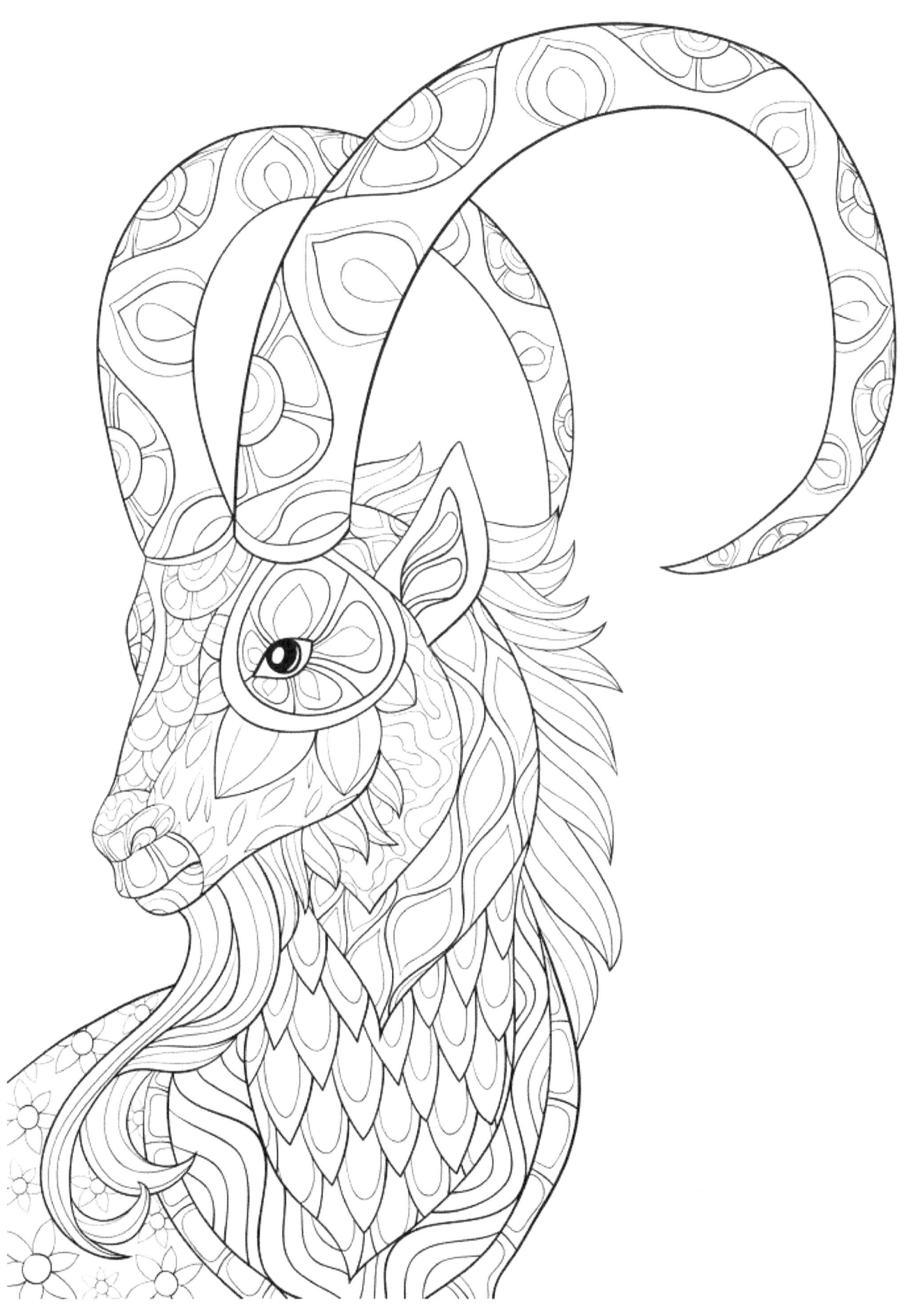

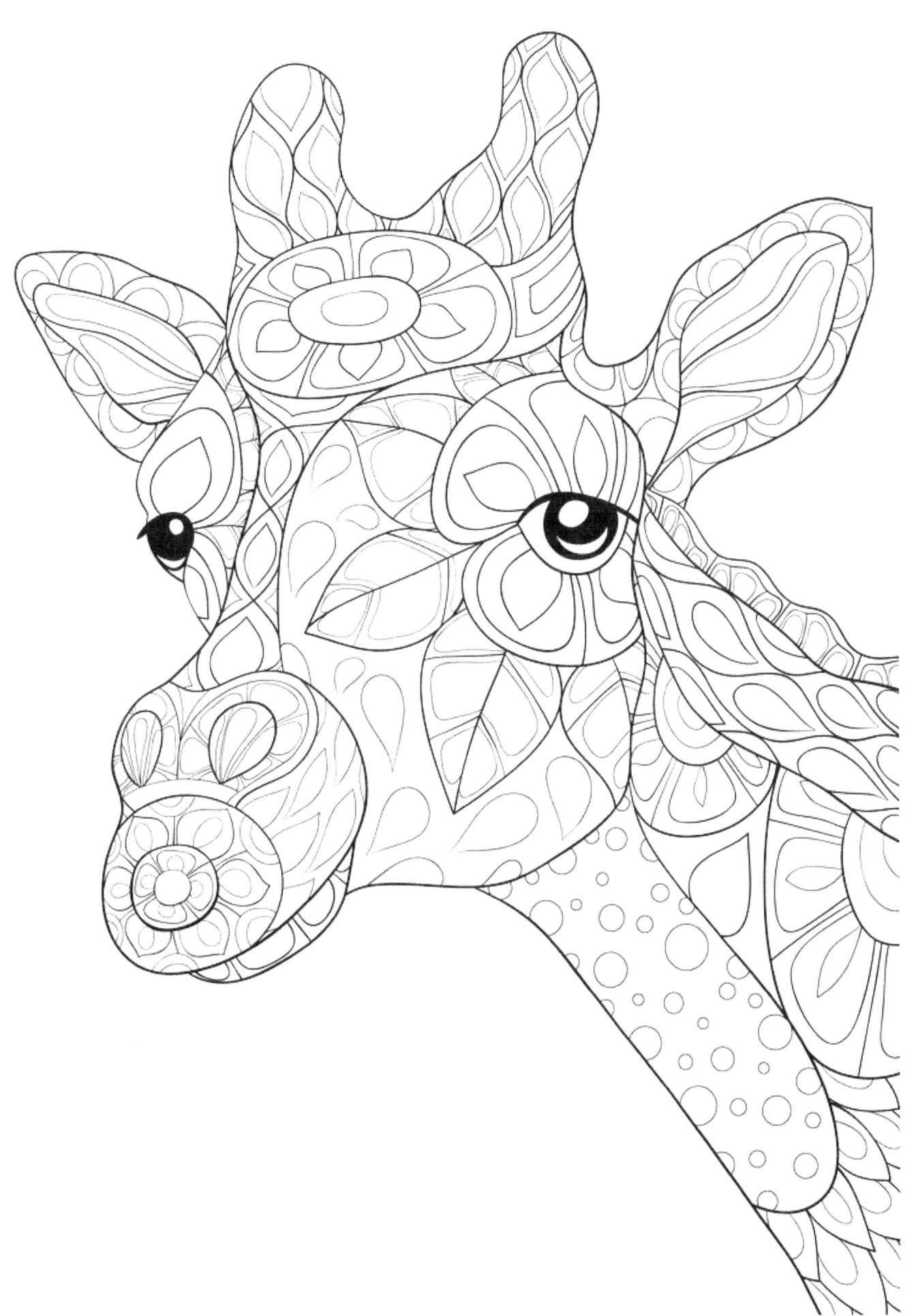

www.ingramcontent.com/pod-product-compliance
Lightning Source LLC
Chambersburg PA
CBHW060412220526
45465CB00008B/2861